White Christmas

White Christmas

DECORATI...   ...DAY SEASON

Clarkson Potter/Publishers
New York

OTHER BOOKS BY TRICIA FOLEY

HAVING TEA

LINENS AND LACE

THE ROMANCE OF
BRITISH COLONIAL STYLE

THE NATURAL HOME

*To my family,
for always being there
and for making
Christmas happen...*

Published by Clarkson N. Potter, Inc.
201 East 50th Street,
New York, New York 10022.
Member of the Crown Publishing Group.

Random House, Inc. New York, Toronto,
London, Sydney, Auckland

http://www.randomhouse.com/

CLARKSON N. POTTER,
POTTER, and colophon are trademarks
of Clarkson N. Potter, Inc.

Printed in China

Design by Douglas Turshen with Nora Negron

Library of Congress Cataloging-in-Publication
Data is available upon request.

ISBN 0-517-70411-0

10 9 8 7 6 5 4 3

Home Made
Plum Pudding

CONTENTS

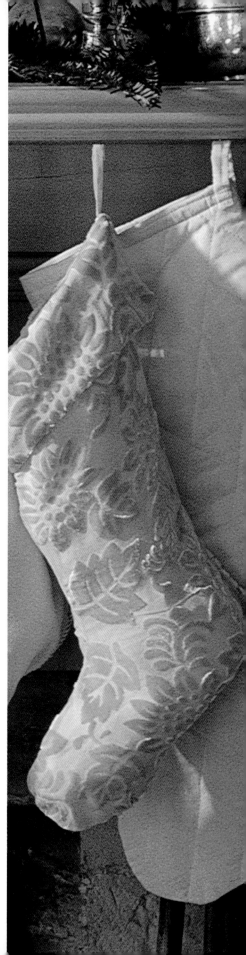

Acknowledgments

I WOULD LIKE TO THANK all those
whose Christmas spirit made this
book come to life: Bill Steele,
for his patience in waiting for the snow
and capturing it so beautifully on
film; Jill Kirchner, whose words are just
right; and Doug Turshen, whose
design expresses this concept so well.

To all those who welcomed
us into their homes over the holidays,
I would like to express my gratitude:
Kristina Ratia, Peri Wolfman,
Matthew Mattiello, Jane and Catherine
of Ornamenta, and my friends at
Meadowcroft and the Hawkins House.
A big thank-you to Paola Sala,
Joan Vass, and Jeannette Marconi, for
creating such luscious stockings;
to Annie Rowland, for her exquisite
calligraphy; to Terri Lucas, for
constructing an all-white gingerbread
mansion for us; to Alexandra Randall,
whose way with flowers is magical;
and to Belle Edsall, for all her help
along the way. A special thank-you to
my family for putting up with all
my unusual requests such as Christmas
trees in March and mittens in June;
to Dennis, for his pickup truck; to
Melissa and Katie, for making the best
angel wings; to Michael and Timothy,
for the excitement in their eyes at
Christmas that makes it all worth it; to
Mary and Kirby, for having the perfect
"Christmas in Connecticut" house;
and to my parents: Dad, for finding my
old-fashioned sled, and Mom, for her
shortbread and crocheted snowflakes.

My appreciation also goes to my
agents Deborah Geltman and Gayle
Benderoff for their continued support
and encouragement, and to all those at
Clarkson Potter who made this book
a reality: Lauren Shakely, Robbin
Gourley, Paula Cohen, Amy Boorstein,
and Joan Denman—thank you again!

And finally, to Claire Whitcomb
and K. C. Witherell, who came up
with this idea one snowy afternoon.

*My twin nephews, Timothy and
Michael, in matching
hand-knit Christmas tree sweaters,
can always be counted on
to help taste-test the cookies.*

PREFACE

HEN I FIRST SAW MY LITTLE clapboard house in the country, I daydreamed of spending the next Christmas there, with the snow falling, the fire burning brightly in the fireplace, and the family settling in around the Christmas tree. . . . I was dreaming of a "White Christmas."

It is now my home, and for many years my family has gathered there on Christmas Eve, our rituals evolving as our numbers have grown. I have had Boxing Day parties on the twenty-sixth in keeping with my English grandmother's tradition, cocktail parties for the office, and long holiday lunches with friends in front of the fire the week between Christmas and New Year's. I love poring over cookbooks and magazine clippings to plan a theme and menu that is different but simple. My own collection of creamware and silver and crystal is brought out and used with a sprig of ivy or rosemary, the fire is laid, and all the candles are lit—on tables, in windows, on mantels.

I am always looking for the perfect gift on my travels and flea market jaunts, and keep a wicker hamper to fill all year round with these finds as well as snips of ribbon, beautiful papers, and cards of all kinds. One quiet weekend after Thanksgiving I pull it all together with favorite carols playing and the fragrance of a pine tree and wreaths throughout the house, which I love. Taking out favorite ornaments brings back memories of Christmas past and I usually have help from my twin nephews in trimming the tree. When the littlest angel is placed on the top, as Michael says, "Now it's really Christmas!"

INTRODUCTION

IKE A CURRIER and Ives print or a snow-capped New England steeple, the image of the perfect white Christmas is firmly etched in our minds. Never mind that it rarely occurs in much of the country—that snow-frosted holiday ideal has stayed as captive in the heart as the tiny scene inside a snow shaker. But more than a climatic condition, a white Christmas is really a state of mind. It represents the magic of Christmas and its still surprising power to transform. Just as a snowfall can suddenly blanket the world in pure white romance, the Christmas season can open up our hearts, illuminate the depths of winter with joy and celebration, and fill us with hope.

The beauty of a snow-white Christmas starts outside—with thick white frosting outlining each bough and branch, drifts of snow softening the edges of the house, and the tiny footprints of birds and the silhouettes of "angels" imprinted in the snow. But I also love the purity and simplicity of a white Christmas inside, captured in a multitude of

Scenes from a white Christmas: A vintage snow shaker, ABOVE, re-creates the magic of a snowfall inside its glass dome. Ice skates saved since high school, RIGHT, are rescued from the back of the closet for a session of skating on a snow-covered pond.

details—a frothy mug of eggnog on Christmas Eve, windows framed in frost or dotted with hand-cut paper snowflakes, the pungent scent of paperwhites, the old-fashioned charm of stockings sewn from old Marseilles spreads and antique lace. The serenity of white brings an elegance and simplicity to holiday decorating. It provides a crisp contrast to fresh greenery, sets a subtle backdrop for shimmering gold and silver accents, and evokes a timeless beauty that endures from year to year.

In this book you'll find a wealth of ways to let the natural simplicity of white inspire every aspect of celebration—from Christmas trees, garlands, and wreaths to heartfelt gifts with homemade wrappings and winter-white table settings and touches of warmth for each room in the house.

Even when we are quite fully grown, there is something about snow—and Christmas—that brings out the child in us. May this book help you remember that magic and re-create it for your own children, and the child in you.

Winter White

White has long been a decorating classic, but it is also well suited to holiday trimmings,

managing to be both elegant and natural at the same time. Shades of white echo

the monochromatic landscape of winter, pale and ethereal as a cloud or a snowdrift.

At Christmastime, the natural palette becomes the velvety greens of fir trees,

ivy, and moss, against which liberal doses of white—in ornaments, flowers, berries, and

and Evergreen

Decorating for Christmas

bows—sparkle and gleam, just as snow sets off the pine trees and bare branches

outside. In addition to snow, nature offers its own shades of white in birch logs and

reindeer moss, tallow berries and narcissus bulbs. Crisp white picket fences

and paneled doors, damask tablecloths and ivory-hued walls show off the beauty of

evergreens to their finest. White brings light—and life—to the darkness inside,

reflecting the twinkle of tree lights and candles, brightening our houses and hopes.

A WREATH OF WELCOME

ASHIONED FROM BOUGHS OF pine or rustic twigs, festooned with berries, clusters of fruit or a magnanimous bow, a wreath is how a house says "welcome." Though found year-round in various forms, wreaths are most closely entwined with Christmas, when they offer signs of life in a wintry landscape and serve as harbingers of cheer indoors as well. Wreaths are as old as ancient Greece, when people wore rings of laurel; they have been used to grace the door and decorate the home at Christmas at least since Victorian times.

Wreaths traditionally form a self-contained circle, though they can be found in square or heart shapes as well, in sizes large to small. The front door certainly deserves one (or two, for French or double doors), but wreaths may adorn other, less expected elements of the home, such as windows, interior doors, armoire or cabinet doors, folding screens, mantels, and headboards. Wreaths may hang in front of a mirror or bookcases; miniatures may dangle from doorknobs or encircle wall sconces.

The base of a wreath may be wire, straw, grapevine, moss, Styrofoam, or florist's foam (which can be soaked in water to extend the life of greens and flowers). A ready-made evergreen wreath can also be used as a starting point for decoration. Affix fresh greens and berries to the base using florists' wire; use florists' picks to attach heavier items such as fruit. Nonliving elements can be hot-glued onto a sturdy straw or Styrofoam base. A wreath can be artfully adorned with bunches of fresh, dried, or faux fruits; stems of flowers, berries, or herbs; or seasonal ornaments and toys. Reindeer moss, winter berries, dried hydrangeas, and ivory roses are favorites of mine for winter-white wreathing. Themed wreaths are particularly charming: A bay leaf wreath dotted with sprigs of herbs, such as sage, rosemary, thyme, and dill, along with peppers, heads of garlic, or tiny onions, makes a useful kitchen wreath. A fragrant wreath for bedroom and bath might feature dried herbs and flowers such as artemisia, lavender, larkspur, rosebuds, and hydrangea.

Even the simplest pine wreath takes on a festive air dressed with a big silk tafetta bow or a sophisticated sheer gold ribbon, though greens or vines left unadorned have a simple eloquence all their own.

Wreaths imbue our homes with the scent and beauty of the season and encircle our hearts with love.

ABOVE: *A trio of boxwood wreaths in descending sizes is joined by ivory wire ribbon to create a striking silhouette in a window. A diminutive wreath of winter-white tallow berries,* RIGHT, *hangs on gossamer ribbon from a screen fashioned from old painted shutters.*

reaths as varied as *the doors they adorn,* CLOCKWISE FROM TOP LEFT: *A brilliant cranberry wreath stands out against a dark green door framed in pine. A rustic grapevine wreath suits this weathered barn. A wreath of evergreen encircles a tiny window in a front door. Boxwood is swagged and wreathed around the top of a panel door. In Sweden, braided straw wreaths like this one are typical. An iron gate is capped with a boxwood garland and wreath. Dried hydrangeas echo the blue-green shade of worn shutters. A rye-grass wreath adorns the doors of a garden house.* LEFT: *Snow crowns a leafy wreath in wonder.*

*P*erched on a
birdbath pedestal, a rye-grass
wreath has a second life
as a feast for feathered friends
in the cold of winter. In the
pantry, RIGHT, a bay-leaf
wreath offers year-round
scent and seasoning for soups
and sauces.

THE HOLLY AND THE IVY

ONG BEFORE THEY were a part of the Christmas celebration, evergreens were a centerpiece of winter solstice festivities, treasured for their seemingly miraculous ability to flourish through the long, cold winter. Today, we revere evergreens no less for their welcome reminder of the outdoors, and of life and rebirth in the darkest depths of winter. Their verdant color and heady fragrance make them a natural choice for decorating in and around the home. Year-round greens such as pine, fir, cedar, spruce, cypress, boxwood, holly, yew, laurel, and juniper are often as close by as your backyard. The woods or the florists are sources for more unusual possibilities, such as eucalyptus pods, poppy flower heads, fig branches, or crab apples.

The uses for greens are as myriad as the different kinds. Garlands and swags of greenery bestow a simple grandeur to porch columns and railings, doorways and windows (indoors and out), mantels and mirrors, banisters and bedposts. Mixing varieties and textures of greenery yields bountiful garlands—white pine with laurel leaves, cedar, or wisps of feathery Princess pine, along with berried branches of juniper or hawthorn. Boxwood roping or strands of ivy can be a fresh alternative to the ubiquitous pine.

Garlands are the ideal frame for architectural

A lush swag of cedar, ABOVE, *mixed with winter berries, dried hydrangea, and pinecones spirals down the base of a pedestal.* RIGHT: *A garland of juniper and eucalyptus drapes a staircase lined with candles.*

elements, but touches of greenery can be nestled into almost any corner: greens and berried sprigs brighten bookshelves or can be tucked behind paintings; boughs can be woven between chandelier arms or candelabras; and branches can be swagged across headboards. Velvety magnolia leaves dress up a mantel, and ivy trailing around a mirror frame gives it a romantic look. For an opulent effect, greens may be garnished with fruits (real or faux), flowers (fresh or dried), pinecones, tiny white lights, or shimmering tendrils of ribbon. Glimmers of white—from statice, larkspur, hydrangea, winter berries—give an elegant, snow-kissed effect. Greenery can also take shape—in the form of myrtle, rosemary, or ivy topiaries; moss-covered balls; or miniature conifers.

Some plants, such as holly and mistletoe, have special meaning at the holidays. In ancient times, holly was believed to be magical because it could bear fruit in winter; people hung it over their beds to inspire sweet dreams. Mistletoe (see box on page 22) was considered sacred for similar reasons, and eventually inspired the custom of kissing beneath a bough hung from a doorway.

Whether mystical or simply enchanting, nature's own finery is often the most beautiful way to fill your home with the spirit of the season.

Gracious Garlands and Swags

FASHIONING BRANCHES of greenery into garlands and swags is easy to do yourself. Use a length of sturdy twine as your base. Gather clusters of greenery together at the stems and lash together with florists' wire. Next affix each bundle to the twine base, taking care to overlap each cluster to conceal the stems and wire.

Anchor the garlands using nails, then drape or wind them around columns, railings, and door frames. Secure where needed with lengths of florists' wire. A less damaging method is to use large white cup hooks, which screw easily into walls and woodwork.

Magnolia leaves are gathered into a genteel garland and wreath, ABOVE. *The leaves are arranged to show the velvety brown undersides as well as the glossy green tops. Garlands of boxwood accented with moiré bows,* RIGHT, *are swagged across porch railings and wound around columns.*

The Kissing Bough

MISTLETOE IS a plant with an illustrious past: It is the Golden Bough of classical legend, picked by Aeneas from an oak tree at the entrance to the underworld. It was considered sacred by the Druids because it grows without roots. Romans hung mistletoe inside to ensure their fields would be fertile again in spring. Mistletoe was also a symbol of peace: Warring soldiers were supposed to lay down their arms beneath mistletoe. Ancient Britons hung it in their doorways to ward off evil; those who entered the house safely were greeted with a kiss. Eventually it became the custom in England and then America to kiss anyone who could be lured beneath the magical bough.

Greens at their simplest:
Boughs of pine are nestled around
white enamelware pitchers,
RIGHT, *and mistletoe tied with a*
bow festoons a sconce, ABOVE.

Making Greens Last

WITH THE PROPER care, garlands, trees, and boughs of fresh evergreens will usually last two to three weeks; berried branches and sturdy leaves such as magnolia and boxwood may last longer, and will usually retain their color as they dry. Keep greens away from radiators and other sources of heat; keep them moist with a humidifier or by misting daily with water. Arrangements of branches and berries should be placed in water; cut, then smash the stems of woody branches to help them absorb water more easily.

ABOVE: *Even a vintage waistcoat can be decked with a sprig of greenery.* RIGHT: *A sleigh bed draped in gauzy netting and outlined in fresh boxwood garlands—the ultimate in Christmas romance.*

O Christmas Tree!

F THERE IS ONE CHRISTMAS custom that shines brightest in our hearts, it is probably decorating the Christmas tree. Setting a majestic freshly cut tree in a corner of the living room, with its graceful boughs stretched outward, perfuming the air with the scent of pine, transforms even the humblest room into an enchanted forest. Whether your preference is for a towering fir or a bushy Scotch pine, each family has its own treasured ritual for selecting a tree. Perhaps one snowy Saturday afternoon it's deemed time for the much-anticipated trip to the tree farm, where little ones can help choose the tree to be cut and then triumphantly transport it home. Or the tree may be a Charlie Brown special, rescued at the last minute from some city sidewalk lot, then taken home to be revived with homemade ornaments and love.

We have the Germans to thank for the tradition of the "Tannenbaum," although theirs were often small tabletop trees, decorated with cookies, fruits, and candies and lit with candles. The Hessian soldiers defeated by George Washington on Christmas in 1776 were probably the first to introduce the custom here, but it failed to catch on until the middle of the nineteenth century. Eventually, the American Christmas tree grew as large in our imaginations as the towering ninety-foot tree in Rockefeller Center, glittering with a dazzling array of lights, or the one that suddenly appears in front of our eyes in *The Nutcracker.*

Just as important as the tree itself are the decorations. Once a year the boxes of ornaments are unearthed from their hiding place in the attic or basement, and the sentimental ritual of unwrapping and hanging the various balls and baubles, each endowed with its own special memories, begins. Every family has its own tree-trimming traditions—watching the film *It's a Wonderful Life* or listening to Nat King Cole's carols, stringing popcorn, or recalling favorite trees of the past. Some people decorate their tree differently each year, devising various themes or color schemes, while many of us have a storehouse of accumulated ornaments that form a sort of family album, hung every year with affectionate repetition. Egg-carton bells made in nursery school may share space with hand-blown glass balls found on travels abroad and gilded globes from generations past. One popular tradition is to buy a new ornament each year or for each of the children; another is to collect according to a certain theme—folk-art creations, silvered glass, or miniature birdhouses.

ABOVE: *Katie gleefully pulls a sled into the fresh-fallen snow.*
RIGHT: *A towering evergreen stands majestically in the woods, its boughs laden with snow. Sometimes our favorite trees are ones we discover and adopt in their natural setting.*

Luminous white ornaments stand out beautifully against plush evergreen branches. Vintage blown-glass balls frosted with "snow," shimmering icicles, pearly white beads, and softly glittering garlands of ribbon create the effect of a snow-dusted tree in the middle of a forest. A folk-art tree brings a more rustic shade of white, with hand-carved wooden snowmen and stars, button-jar angels, crocheted mittens, and hearts wrought from grapevines. Nature's contributions to an all-white tree might be gifts from the sea—sun-bleached scallop shells and aptly shaped starfish, rare sea-horses and pearl-studded conch shells; or woodsier finds—white-painted pinecones, lichen and reindeer moss, balls covered in winter berries. Then again, sometimes a simple, unadorned tree is the most beautiful of all.

The tree stand need not be an afterthought; there are many attractive possibilities beyond the standard

ABOVE: *An evergreen wreath brightens the bumper of my brother Dennis's 1954 Chevy pickup truck. The children—Melissa, Michael, Katie, and Timmy—load the carefully chosen Christmas tree into the truck,* RIGHT.

metal contraption: A galvanized tub, cast-iron urn, large terra-cotta pot, or wicker basket can hold the tree, anchored with rocks or bricks, then covered with moss, pinecones, or silver balls to conceal the weights. Tree skirts also offer artful camouflage. In addition to the traditional round skirt, other options can be easily improvised: a Marseilles bedspread or country quilt, an old throw or woolen blanket, a covering fashioned from a length of quilted muslin or white flannel, or a pouf of gauze for an ethereal effect.

Beyond all the tinsel and glitter, sometimes our sentimental favorites are our first trees, the ones we dress with sheer ingenuity for lack of traditional ornaments, hanging children's toys, handmade paper snowflakes, or bundles of cinnamon sticks as decoration. Each year, we build on the Christmas trees of our memories, always hoping to create the tree of our dreams.

A Guide to Trees

FIR TREES HAVE short, soft, dark green needles and a symmetrical shape, although the branches are usually irregularly spaced. Firs have excellent needle retention and Balsam firs in particular are very fragrant.

Eastern White or Scotch pines have clusters of long, thin blue-green needles and a bushy, conical shape. Scotch pines have the best needle retention.

Spruce trees usually have a bluish cast, with sharp, dense needles and strong branches, but lose their needles more quickly. The slightly drooping branches of Norway spruces have a dramatic look but are harder to decorate.

FOR THE FRESHEST tree, purchase directly from a tree farm. If you buy from a lot, try these tests for freshness:

Bend the branches as well as individual needles to make sure they are flexible. Bounce the tree on its stump one or two times —some needles will invariably fall off, but there shouldn't be an avalanche. The trunk should still be sticky with sap.

Once you get the tree home, recut an inch off the bottom of the trunk and place it in warm water right away. Keep it in a cool place, away from heaters, and refill the water often: Trees can drink as much as a gallon a day.

INVESTING IN A live tree is a tradition that lives on after the holidays. Dig a hole for the tree before the ground freezes. When you get the tree home, leave it in the garage for a couple days to acclimatize it to indoor temperatures. Then place it in a large washtub anchored with rocks. Keep it indoors for just a week or less. After Christmas, recondition it to colder weather again in the garage or basement. Plant it in the predug hole, removing the root ball wrapping and loosening the roots with a garden fork. Pack down soil and mulch around the roots, and water it well.

*Touches of gold—
shimmering garlands of ribbon
and light-catching balls—
illuminate the Christmas tree,
anchored in an earthenware
bread bowl. Boxwood
roping frames the room's entry.*

sampler of ornaments, old and new, CLOCKWISE FROM TOP LEFT: *A handblown glass ball with silver leafing. A tiny hand-knit mitten. A painted glass Christmas tree is a clip-on ornament from the turn of the century. A heart-shaped button angel. In rustic wood, a primitive white-washed star. The snow-dusted pear recalls a familiar holiday symbol. Simple twigs, tied in the shape of a heart. A knitted bootie pays sentimental tribute to a baby's first Christmas.*

Ornaments to treasure, CLOCKWISE FROM TOP LEFT: *A humble wooden snowman is hung by a loop of wire. This embossed silver ball is probably from the 1930s. A man-made nest cradles a bird's egg. All-natural: a ball covered in seeds and tied with raffia. A hand-crocheted heart. A delicate silver ball from the 1920s. This folk-art snowman is made from wool flannel with clove buttons. Seaside inspiration: A scallop shell becomes an ornament.*

Silvered balls, glittering glass beads, and crystal prisms sparkle on a lush, round tree filling a corner of a living room, RIGHT. *Child-size wooden horses flank the tree, along with small Swedish chairs proffering presents (more miniatures perch atop the bookshelves).* THIS PAGE: *The silvery glow extends to the mantel, with mercury glass balls and a glass-beaded candelabra reflected in the mirror. Boxwood topiaries nestled in silvered pots add a touch of greenery.*

*T*he Christmas tree, LEFT, has been coated in spray snow giving it a wintry effect that echoes the frosted and pearlized ornaments on its branches. CLOCKWISE FROM TOP: A pinecone adorned with seeds and berries is frosted with snow and hung by thin cord. Vintage pinecone ornaments and mercury glass balls are stored in a wicker basket filled with straw—an easy, all-natural way to cushion fragile decorations. A striped teardrop-shaped glass ornament is tied onto a tree branch with ribbon. Snow-dusted glass icicles catch the light. A new pressed tin teapot ornament adds to the silvery theme.

The First Christmas Ornaments

I N MEDIEVAL TIMES, red apples were hung on evergreen trees to celebrate "Adam and Eve Day" on December twenty-fourth. The first Christmas tree ornaments, appearing in Germany in the seventeenth century, were handmade from paper or edible treats such as fruits and bonbons; eventually small gifts were hung on the tree as well (in some countries, Saint Nicholas leaves gifts on the tree). Candles were affixed to the branches and lit on Christmas Eve. In the 1870s, Germany began making and selling heavy handblown glass globes known as Kugels, hand-cast lead ornaments, and Dresdens, elaborately gilded cardboard ornaments. The end of the nineteenth century also saw the introduction of foil icicles, "angel hair" made from spun glass, and tinsel garlands. In the 1890s, tree lights became the safer alternative to candles. By 1940 machine-made Christmas balls had inundated the market, and handblown glass ornaments became a rarity. They're highly sought-after today as collectors' items.

Make Your Own Pomanders

Mix together equal parts of ground cinnamon, nutmeg, cloves, and orris root powder in a mixing bowl.

Stud lemons or oranges with whole cloves. (Use a knitting needle to puncture the fruit first to make inserting the cloves easier.) Patterns can be created with the cloves—spirals, swirls, horizontal or vertical stripes, borders, or plaids. Put the clove-studded fruit in a mixing bowl and cover with the spice mixture by stirring with a wooden spoon.

Leave the fruit for two weeks or more, stirring and rotating daily to coat the fruit evenly.

Tie with raffia, silk cord and tassels, or velvet or taffeta ribbons to hang on the tree or a door-knob. Or put in bowls or use on tables or mantels as a still life.

LEFT, *a clove-studded pomander is wrapped in organdy ribbon to be hung from a doorway or tree. A box of memories,* RIGHT, *holds vintage ornaments from the 1930s and 40s glass and metal balls in pearlized and metallic finishes.*

WINTER BLOOMS

O SEE A FLOWER BLOOMING in the midst of winter is nothing short of miraculous: The luxury of their fragile, evanescent beauty awakens our soul to the possibility of spring during the dreariness of winter's fallow days. Against a background of hearty greenery—pine and fir branches, holly and juniper boughs—delicate white blossoms offer a tender contrast of texture and fragrance.

Some flowers are associated with the season because they have the rare distinction of blooming in winter, such as the Christmas rose (*Helleborus niger*), with its dainty white petals and yellow stamens. The ubiquitous poinsettia, a Christmas cliché in red, becomes sophisticated in ivory. Other traditional favorites, such as paperwhites and amaryllis, can easily be forced from bulbs in winter, while hothouse- or

Pots of paperwhite bulbs, ABOVE, *aren't quite in bloom yet, but the pleasure is in watching them come into flower.* RIGHT: *A butler's tray serves up bulbs forced into flower— hyacinths and amaryllis— along with a norfolk pine seedling.*

foreign-grown roses and tulips are now available year-round at flower markets.

Many Christmas flowers have a particular symbolism or legend attached to them: The trumpetlike shape of the amaryllis is said to symbolize the horn blown by an archangel to herald the birth of Christ. The star that guided the Wise Men, so it is told, burst into the constellation of tiny flowers called star-of-Bethlehem. And according to Mexican legend, when a poor boy had no gift to bring to the church on Christmas Eve, a poinsettia miraculously grew on the spot outside where he knelt to pray.

Whether a single dramatic stalk of amaryllis or a cluster of tiny snowdrops, white flowers bring an element of elegance to holiday decorating. White is refreshing, romantic, and refined.

Forcing Bulbs for Christmas

BULBS CAN BE found at nurseries or through garden catalogs. You'll also need gravel or pebbles, potting soil, and terra-cotta pots or other containers. (For wooden crates, line with plastic, then fill with soil.)

Among the simplest bulbs to grow are those that do not need a long period of chilling, such as paperwhites. Start four to six weeks in advance of desired blooming. Cover any drainage holes with pottery shards and fill the pot two-thirds full with gravel or potting soil. Place the bulbs in the pot pointed end up, close together but not touching, then fill in around

them. Water to the bottom of the bulbs. Keep the pot in a cool, dark place like a refrigerator, basement, or garage. When roots have developed—in two to three weeks—move the container to a cool sunny spot, such as a windowsill. Within three weeks you'll have fragrant white blossoms.

Pure white berries and blooms stand in clean relief against boughs of evergreens; the faded translucency of dried white flowers such as hydrangea blossoms or honeycombed reindeer moss offers a subtler charm. Roses add beauty to a table in the soft blush of candlelight and bring a painterly grace to a grouping of fruits or greens.

Bulbs can be bought already forced and in flower, but it is more rewarding (and less expensive) to start them yourself and follow their steady progress as they unfurl and bloom (see box on page 40). Topiaries and flowering plants such as orchids also offer long-lasting pleasure.

Flowers fill a home with hospitality and make a generous gift of welcome or thanks throughout the season.

Scents of the Season

THERE IS AN OLD saying that if you burn a bayberry candle on Christmas Eve, you will have good luck the whole year long. Like bayberry, there are a whole host of scents associated with the holidays—pine and cedar; cinnamon, vanilla, nutmeg, and clove; juniper and rosemary. Enhance the sensory experience of the holidays with candles lightly fragranced with vanilla or cypress; orange pomanders studded with cloves; natural potpourri made from pine needles, juniper berries, cinnamon sticks, allspice berries, and star anise. Or make mulling spices or a simmering potpourri on the stove with cinnamon, cloves, orange peel, and bay leaves.

An abundance of sweet-scented paperwhites, ABOVE, *fills a terra-cotta pot to overflowing. A bouquet of tulips wrapped in cellophane,* LEFT, *spills out of a natural-wool stocking.* RIGHT: *Whisper-pale roses are tucked into candlesticks and clustered into a shapely porcelain vase.*

CANDLE GLOW AND FIRELIGHT

ONG BEFORE there were electric lights, candles brought light and a reminder of the sun during the long dark winter. But even now, in the shelter of our lamp-lit homes, candles retain a quiet power and a magical beauty that artificial lighting cannot equal.

Candles play an important role in both Hanukkah, the festival of lights of Jewish tradition, and Christmas. Once a part of pagan ritual, in the Christian church, candles came to represent the light of Christ. In medieval times, it was customary to light a candle on Christmas that, tended with care, would last until Twelfth Night. Candles are also used to mark the coming of Christmas on the Advent wreath. Starting the fourth Sunday before Christmas, one candle is lit each Sunday until Christmas Eve, when all five candles are illuminated. Before the introduction of electric lights, candles were used to light the Christmas tree. Legend (probably apocryphal) tells of Martin Luther walking in the woods one Christmas Eve and being so overcome with the beauty of God's handiwork—the stars lighting up the heavens and the boughs of the evergreen trees below—that he cut down a tree, brought it home, and lit it with candles to try to re-create the wondrous sight for his family.

Candlelight is one of the most beautiful and easi-

To brighten dark winter nights, ABOVE, *a candle sconce with mirrored tiles reflects light into the room. An elegant assortment of ceramic and silver candlesticks,* RIGHT, *illuminates a table.*

est ways to create a sense of special occasion in any room. A grouping of candlesticks with a variety of silhouettes—in gleaming silver, pure white ironstone, sparkling crystal, or rich wood—creates an interesting composition of form and a halo of light that becomes an immediate focal point. Candlelight invites attention to whatever is placed beside it—flowers, greenery, or food. Votives lined along a windowsill bring warmth to a cold, dark void of glass; placed on a tray, they can light up a non-working fireplace. Pillars of varying heights can be grouped among greens and fruits for a natural mantel- or centerpiece. A mirror multiplies the glow of a candle, as do shimmering candleholders of glass, silver, or tin. Sconces and chandeliers fitted with candles rather than bulbs have an old-fashioned elegance and warmth, and fill a room with a soft, ambient glow.

White or ivory candles are a classic choice. Beeswax has a pleasant natural fragrance and doesn't drip as it burns, though it tends to burn more quickly than conventional paraffin. Tapers encircled with a small wreath of berries, boxwood, ivy, or rosemary or candleholders tucked with sprigs of pine or holly add a dash of holiday spirit.

The light of the wood fire is another way to warm the heart and soul at Christmastime. Druids and Celts

burned large bonfires during the winter solstice (the shortest day of the year) in hopes of luring back the sun. Eventually, the tradition evolved into the lighting of the yule log, lit on Christmas Eve and burned throughout the twelve days of Christmas. Traditionally, a piece of the previous year's log is used to light the new log. In some parts of France, children believe that the yule log is the source of their gifts; it is also re-created in the *bûche de Noël,* a rolled cake filled and iced with chocolate buttercream to resemble a log, then studded with meringue "mushrooms."

The best place to be on a cold, snowy eve is still in front of the brilliant flames and crackling roar of a fire, warming one's toes while sipping hot cocoa and dreaming of Christmases past and those to come.

*C*andles light up a home. FAR LEFT, CLOCKWISE FROM TOP: *A wreath of Swedish ivy adorns a gilded mirror and sconce. Silver candlesticks reflect the light. Glass hurricanes protect flames from drafts. A bedside candle encircled in boxwood.*

THIS PAGE, CLOCKWISE FROM TOP LEFT: *Candlesticks festively ringed in berries. A mantel is lit by sconces and candlesticks. Santa's slippers by the fire. This glass candleholder can be hung from a window or a tree. Bundles of white tapers are tied with sprigs of greenery. A moiré bow and eucalyptus bedeck a silver sconce.*

Timeless

Even for those who shun tradition and ritual the rest of the year, Christmas is

one time we often return to the security of its fold. Holiday traditions resonate with the

imprimatur of time; they become a part of our identity, writing our family history

and reflecting our cultural heritage. Cards and greetings are often still hand-penned

and sent by post; stockings are hung by the chimney on Christmas Eve; gifts are

Traditions

THE CUSTOMS OF CHRISTMAS

carefully chosen, wrapped, and beribboned; and Santa still embodies all the fantasies

of children. Snow is still hoped for—and sometimes even received—on Christmas.

White envelops the customs of the season in a mantle of serenity and elegance.

As we seek to put our own stamp on tradition and imbue celebrations with our own

sense of style, the versatility of white becomes an asset: It is a classic that has

stood the test of time, yet easily lends itself to reinvention.

SEASON'S
GREETINGS

NE OF THE FIRST, and most welcome, harbingers of the holiday season is the arrival of Christmas cards in the mailbox. Despite the omnipresence of the fax, e-mail, and telephone, we still treasure the custom of sending personal greetings to families and friends at Christmastime. Whether it is a photo card that shows just how big the children have grown, a handmade card whose thoughtfulness is embedded in its artistry, a long, chatty letter to a much-missed friend, or just a postcard with a heartfelt "Thinking of you!" scrawled on the back, a Christmas card engenders a sense of connection. One winter's afternoon we sit down with a cup of tea, our cards and address file, and we take the time to catch up with old friends

Inviting ways to display and enjoy Christmas cards throughout the season: ABOVE, *a silver toast rack is put to new use serving holiday greetings.* RIGHT, *notes and cards are tucked into the edges of an entry-hall mirror surrounded by small gifts.*

and memories of Christmases past, adding new friends to the list. The chance to "visit," if only in spirit, with the people who are important to us makes this holiday custom particularly meaningful.

White and ivory lend a crisp elegance to Christmas correspondence, whether with traditional engraving, computer-generated type, or old-fashioned calligraphy; antique lithographs or contemporary black-and-white photos. Simple motifs can be photocopied or hand-stamped onto cards, or a family portrait can be mounted onto card stock. Including a newsletter, favorite poem, or family recipe are all ways to add a more personal touch.

The first Christmas card is thought to have been sent by Sir Henry Cole in England in 1843, who, like many modern-day correspondents, was late in writing his holiday letters and asked an artist friend to design a card that he could send instead. The Christmas card was born, and soon the Victorians were eagerly printing up and sending beautifully illustrated cards by the thousands. At the height of their popularity in the 1880s and 1890s, there were more than 200,000 different designs to choose from. Many of the favored images were naturalistic themes such as snowy winter landscapes, animals, and birds—in particular robins, who were associated both with Christmas legend and with British postmen, who wore red uniforms. Popular novelties included elaborate pop-up, embossed, and fabric-trimmed cards. In the United States, Boston printer Louis Prang began offering colored lithograph cards in 1875, and their artistically rendered designs became widely popular. It wasn't until 1962 that special Christmas postage stamps were offered in the United States; they are now among the postal service's best-sellers.

The rich assortment of cards sent is also a resource for holiday decorating when displayed as a reminder of far-off friends and family. There are the traditional methods of display, such as pinning cards to lengths of velvet or satin ribbon or propping them on the mantel, but fresher approaches abound as well: tucking cards into the edges of a gilded mirror, much as English country house mirrors often held a cache of invitations, or slipping them into a memory board—a prettier version of a fabric-covered bulletin board, with crisscrossed ribbons. Cards can be tacked up on a folding screen, served up on a tray atop a coffee table, or lined up in a silver toast rack.

Once the season is over, treasured images gain a second life clipped out with pinking or scalloped-edge shears and recycled as gift tags the next year. Cards with special meaning can be bundled together with ribbon or glued into a scrapbook or album and saved to cheer a rainy afternoon.

In an age of instant, disposable communication, Christmas cards are all the more valuable for the time and thoughtful spirit they embody.

A treasured vintage card, ABOVE, *is hung from the edge of a folding screen. A memory board,* LEFT, *holds cards, photos, and seasonal mementos without damaging them. The fabric-covered bulletin board has been crisscrossed with ribbons tacked into place to form a lattice; cards can then simply be tucked beneath the ribbons.* BELOW, *old-fashioned calligraphy adds a personal touch to holiday correspondence, invitations, and special enclosures.*

STOCKINGS HUNG WITH CARE

OR A CHILD, CHRISTMAS morning is a time of absolute magic: Having barely slept a wink the night before, what with all the excitement and straining to hear reindeers' hooves on the roof, they awaken at dawn and begin the campaign to convince their parents that it is time to get up. Finally, the pajama-clad pilgrimage downstairs begins, eyes wide with anticipation to see what Santa has brought. And although there may be large packages piled up beneath the tree, first comes something just as special on a miniature scale: the Christmas stocking. Empty the eve before, the stockings are now bulging with toys and treats. In the book *Mrs. Miniver,* written in 1939, Jan Struther captures the timeless appeal of the Christmas stocking: "Perhaps it was the charm of the miniature, of toy toys, of smallness squared; perhaps it was the sense of limitation within a strict form, which gives to both the filler and the emptier of a Christmas stocking something of the same enjoyment which is experienced by the writer and the reader of a sonnet . . . ."

The custom of filling stockings with small gifts is believed to have descended from the original Saint Nicholas, a bishop in Asia Minor in the fourth century. According to legend, he tossed three bags of gold through the window of a destitute family whose three daughters had no dowries and were to be sold into slavery. The gold is said to have landed in the girls' stockings, which had been hung by the fire to dry. Thus we hang our Christmas stockings by the chimney, Santa Claus's traditional route into the house. The stocking ritual also probably derived from the Dutch custom of leaving out wooden shoes to be filled on Saint Nicholas Day, December 6. The original stocking stuffers were usually an orange or apple (rare treats a century ago), walnuts, homemade candies or cookies, perhaps a small toy, chocolate coins (to commemorate St. Nicholas's gift), and a silver quarter. For children who had been naughty, there would be only a rod (for spankings). Nowadays, a lump of coal is threatened as a punishment, but it was once included in stockings to symbolize warmth.

A lacy crocheted stocking from the 1930s, ABOVE, *stands out against evergreen branches. Stockings handmade from old Marseilles bedspreads,* RIGHT, *and topped with crocheted lace have a subtle white-on-white elegance; tendrils of ivy peek out from their tops.*

Real socks, often trimmed and embroidered, were originally used as Christmas stockings, but now they are likely to be specially made for the occasion from wool, felt, needlepoint, velvet, or other fabric. Knitting or stitching a stocking by hand makes a wonderful and generous gift, appreciated year after year as it is proudly hung on the mantel. Stockings made from a favorite fabric, perhaps an old quilt

have nostalgic references that enhance their value; appliqué, embroidery, fringe, and lace add luxury to plainer fabrics. When a new child is born or a new person becomes a part of the family, it is a welcoming gesture to present them with a stocking in keeping with your own family's traditions.

Even in a color palette of white and ivory, there are a wide range of options—from a hand-knit stocking to one of woven felt. The fabric may be humble muslin or elegant cut velvet, but they each offer something unique while maintaining a harmonious design scheme.

Stocking stuffers are still intended to be small treats or unexpected trifles, but they can be just as charming and creative as larger gifts. As we learned early on from our Christmas stockings, the best gifts often come in small packages.

All-white stockings, FROM LEFT: *An angora and mohair stocking with pom-poms, hand-knit by designer Joan Vass; tucked and pleated Irish linen; checkerboard cotton damask with a deep cuff. Old buttons line the cuff of a cotton flannel stocking; felt crimped with pinking shears is woven into a basketweave pattern; a child's stocking made from a Marseilles spread with vintage lace trim. Cotton velvet is piped in silk braid; elegant embossed cut velvet; and simple diamond-quilted muslin.*

WINTER-WHITE GIFT WRAPS

T THE HEART of Christmas is giving. We may bemoan the commercialism of the holidays, but generosity still underlies the essence of Christmas. As adults, we recognize the pleasure in choosing a present we hope will delight the recipient and take joy in bestowing it.

The best gifts are little luxuries that invite relaxation, introspection, joy—whether it be a delicious tea, a cache of scented candles, a beautiful journal or a set of watercolors. Homemade gifts are invested with thoughtfulness, and they need not be time-consuming to make—oils and vinegars seasoned with berries or herbs, sugar flavored with vanilla beans to savor with coffee or tea, a cassette tape of music culled from your personal collection. A gift that reflects a favorite activity —museum memberships, movie passes, magazine subscriptions, tennis-court time, cooking lessons—shows you have been attentive to a friend's interests. Photographs—old or new, framed, or organized into a calendar or small album—are invariably treasured. And, of course, the most valuable gifts needn't cost a penny—an offer to baby-sit, coupons for car washes or dog walking, a scrapbook of Christmas memories.

However simple or small the gift, beautiful wrapping makes it more special; the packaging becomes part of the present. A silk scarf or velvet sack, a Shaker box or simple basket can be both

Well-wrapped, ABOVE: A muslin sack cinched with greens; white paper folded into tuxedo-shirt pleats; dime-store letters spell "peace." Berries bedeck gifts wrapped in quilted paper, RIGHT.

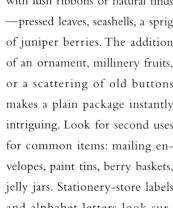

wrapping and gift. Nice wrappings beget creative recycling, so that the box, bow, or tin gets used over and over again. The simplest of materials can make surprisingly elegant wraps: butcher's paper, rice paper, scraps of wallpaper, clear cellophane, even paper bags become something special with a sealing-wax closure or glittering bow.

An all-white or natural palette makes for a sophisticated scheme, which can be tastefully embellished with lush ribbons or natural finds —pressed leaves, seashells, a sprig of juniper berries. The addition of an ornament, millinery fruits, or a scattering of old buttons makes a plain package instantly intriguing. Look for second uses for common items: mailing envelopes, paint tins, berry baskets, jelly jars. Stationery-store labels and alphabet letters look surprisingly chic in gold or silver on glossy white paper. Hard-to-wrap items can be sheathed in fabric, tucked into baskets, or encased in cellophane or netting. Simple sacks sewn from muslin, damask, or velvet make a bottle of wine or champagne an occasion and can be reused for other gifts or even as shoe bags. Craft personalized gift tags from cutout images, photocopies of black and white pictures, recycled greeting cards, or decorate plain card stock with stickers, labels, or rubber stamps.

With a hint of creativity, planning, shopping, and wrapping become enjoyable pursuits.

imple materials, distinctive wraps. TOP LEFT: *Embossed Anaglypta wallpaper; leaf-printed paper tied with cotton twill tape; sheer ribbon printed with pine branches.* TOP RIGHT: *Shaker boxes tied with holly and a paper pocket sealed with wax package table gifts.* BOTTOM LEFT: *A moss-covered box topped with a bouquet.* BOTTOM RIGHT: *Baskets are ideal for hard-to-wrap gifts.* FAR RIGHT: *Lavish ribbon dresses up a simple package; a gift is wrapped in silk cloth, Japanese-style; buttons adorn a small box.*

THE FIRST SNOWFALL

IT STARTS WITH THE QUIET hush that of a world wrapped in a winter blanket. Next, a tentative glimpse out the window, and the revelation that everything has suddenly been painted a heavenly white, with only the faintest of outlines revealing the original forms. Finally, the tiny thrill of realization seeps in that overnight it has snowed and the landscape has been transformed with rare beauty. Each tree branch has been limned in white, each shingle has been dusted with powder, each lamppost topped with a jaunty cap of snow. The snow is still pure and untouched, with only a scattering of footprints plumbing its depths.

For children, snow offers the often prayed-for hope of school being canceled and a sudden day of freedom, filled with the promise of play and excitement. Snow is nature's ultimate toy—a substance to be molded into snowballs and built into igloos and forts, to sail across in a sled, to lie down in and carve out a snow angel, or even to eat! Children join forces for the collaborative venture of sculpting a snowman, winding yarns of snow into massive boulders, stacking them one upon another, and creating a character out of the traditional charcoal, carrot, and scarf or something more inventive. There is the excitement of tobogganing or sledding down a steep, bumpy hill or skating across a frozen pond edged in snow.

There are also the quieter pleasures of filling the feeders for the birds, putting out a salt lick for deer, softly walking and patiently watching to see what the white backdrop reveals in the natural landscape.

After the chill has seeped into the bones or the clothes are soaked with snow, there is the satisfying reward of returning back to a cozy, warm home, with a fire going in the fireplace, a mug of hot cocoa, and the chance to pop popcorn or make cookies.

For adults, an unexpected day of freedom also invites indulging in the indoor pleasures we too rarely allow ourselves—picking up the knitting, writing a letter to a friend, delving into a novel or jigsaw puzzle. Sometimes even the ritual of shoveling snow can be satisfying. When the hectic pace of the workaday world is stilled by a snowfall, it reminds us that there can also be peacefulness and serenity in the world.

Let It Snow!

DON'T BE DISAPPOINTED if it doesn't snow at Christmas. Except in the northernmost latitudes, white Christmases are actually quite a rarity. According to the *New York Times,* there have been only eight in the New York area since 1870, with three in the first decade of this century. From 1909 to 1961, there was not one truly white Christmas.

Farmers' folklore says it will be a snowy winter if birds build their nests high off the ground or if there's more wool than usual on the caterpillars' backs.

Old proverbs claim that the day of the first snow will determine the number of snowfalls that winter or that there will be as many snows as there are frogs in the month of August!

A snowflake is born 5,000 to 10,000 feet above the earth. It is made up of ice crystals that are perfectly clear, but they reflect the light shining on them. The light is refracted into so many different colors that the overall effect is white.

*Snow offers an instant invitation
to play: to build a snowman
with its own unique character,* ABOVE,
*or lie down in the snow
and, with a swish of arms and legs,
become an angel.*

Home for

Food is at the center of many of our most cherished holidays, and Christmas

is no exception—magical once-a-year treats, hallowed recipes passed down from

great-grandmothers, and dishes that connect us to our cultures are all relished this time.

From the cookie baking that starts weeks ahead of time to the Christmas feast,

culinary traditions abound. Entertaining takes on special importance as family and

the Holidays

CHRISTMAS ENTERTAINING

friends are reunited, and pride is taken in the effort to create a special meal or

memorable party. White becomes a welcome simplifier, setting the style as

well as the menu. Sugary white confections set sugar plums dancing in our heads;

creamy soups and breads warm the soul; powdery flourishes top off an

elegant tea. An all-white table can be daintily old-fashioned or cleanly modern,

but it sets an idyllic backdrop that lets the food shine.

VISIONS OF
SUGARPLUMS

IKE PROUST'S famed madeleine, the taste and aroma of certain foods are inextricably linked with the holidays: a whiff of gingerbread cookies baking in the oven, a mug of mulled cider, or a lick of peppermint candy cane can immediately conjure up "Christmas" in our minds. Foods are an integral part of the holidays, with many reserved for and savored only at this time of year: a sugarplum heaven of Christmas cookies, from *pfeffernusse* to sugar cookies to *springerle;* the traditional fruitcake and stollen; spiced wassail and eggnog; chestnuts "roasting on an open fire" or mixed into the dressing. The Christmas dinner, a lavish array of a dozen or more dishes in Victorian times, has been a centerpiece of the holiday celebration almost since its inception. Food forms the foundation of many family traditions, with treasured recipes handed down through generations, a Christmas dinner menu that rarely (if ever) varies, and rituals of cookie making and eggnog mixing that bring family members together.

Though we may buy ready-made sweets or watch our waistlines the rest of the year, for most of us, it wouldn't be Christmas without homemade cookies. Childhood memories of baking with our mother or grandmother, licking the beaters if we were lucky, and carefully decorating each cookie with colored icing, sugar sprinkles, cinnamon hearts, and silver dragees, are etched in our memories of holiday joy. Baking Christmas cookies is one of those tasks where the pleasure of preparation almost equals the tasty delight of consumption.

Homemade plum puddings, a traditional English treat, are packed in ceramic bowls to give as gifts, ABOVE. *Gingerbread,* RIGHT, *has been used to celebrate the holiday for centuries; these crisp smiling gingermen are bound to disappear quickly.*

Like so many holiday traditions, the earliest Christmas cookies, *lebkuchen* and *springerle,* came from Germany. *Springerle*—anise-flavored cookies baked in special molds—date back to pagan winter festivals when they were stamped with images of gods, animals, or other symbols representing sacrifice or fertility. *Lebkuchen,* honey-spice cookies, are shaped into hearts or stars or fashioned into gingerbread houses. Each country has its own favorite variation on the gingerbread cookie: In Belgium, the holiday cookies are *speculaas,* thin, buttery spice cookies molded into Christmas symbols and served on St. Nicholas Day (December sixth). In Sweden, it's *pepparkakor,* heart-shaped gingersnaps. Moravian spice cookies are paper-thin crisps. The English, who introduced gingerbread to America, make a cake that is dark, moist, and studded with candied fruit.

Gingerbread houses, fantasy confections coated with frosting "snow" and outlined in gumdrops,

nonpareils, and other candies, became popular in the early 1800s, after the Brothers Grimm published their fairy tale "Hansel and Gretel," featuring a witch's cottage covered in candy. Ginger abodes have since assumed fanciful proportions as grand architectural creations, but the lure of a house, however humble, made entirely of sweets will always persist.

Not all holiday cookies are ginger-based, of course. There are anise-flavored cookies (such as *bizcochitos* from New Mexico), cinnamon stars (an Alsatian specialty, served on Christmas Eve), almond

ced sugar-cookie angels, ABOVE, are pretty enough to hang on the tree. The fantastical gingerbread house, RIGHT, with its seed-shingled roof, is a copy of a Victorian house in New York.

crescents, pecan balls, Italian hazelnut cookies, cookie-cutter sugar cookies, shortbread, meringues, and more. Give any cookie a snow-dusted effect with a sprinkling of confectioners' sugar or coconut, a glaze of icing, or piped-on details in white frosting, accented with shimmering silver dragees. Another special effect is to sift confectioners' sugar onto chocolate or gingerbread cookies through a stencil to create a snowflake or other pattern.

Fruitcake and plum pudding, traditional English holiday sweets, are not as revered on this side of the

Sweet Traditions: Santa Lucia Day

IN THE EARLY morning on December thirteenth, Swedish girls dressed in long white gowns and a crown of candles serve their mothers breakfast in bed. Special songs are sung, and the girls serve saffron buns (called *lussekatter* because they look like cat's eyes) and gingerbread biscuits with coffee and perhaps glogg (pronounced "glug"), a mulled wine. The day is also celebrated in the community, with Santa Lucias leading processions of girls singing carols.

Pepparkakor, or gingersnaps, ABOVE, *are heart-shaped cookies made in honor of St. Lucia's Day in Sweden. Dried fruits,* RIGHT, *are one of thirteen desserts served for the Reveillon in France.*

Atlantic as cookies, but when well made, they are delicious desserts with a long heritage. Plum pudding or figgy pudding, immortalized by Dickens and in carols, is a steamed pudding made with dried fruits (raisins were once called "plums"), nuts, eggs, spices, brown sugar, and suet. It is traditionally made weeks or even months in advance, preserved in a brandy-soaked cloth, and served hot, usually with a hard sauce made of butter, sugar, and brandy or cognac. For Christmas or Twelfth Night (January fifth, the eve of Epiphany), a small silver charm or sixpence is baked into the pudding; it's believed whoever finds it will have good fortune. Fruitcake is

made with similar ingredients, including dried or candied fruits, nuts, and liquor, and if prepared correctly, produces a dense, moist loaf. In France, the ceremonial desserts are both more luscious and whimsical: the *croquembouche,* a towering mass of cream puffs stacked into a cone shape and wrapped in a web of spun sugar, and the *bûche de Nöel,* a rich, cream-filled cake shaped like the yule log.

To truly sate the sweet tooth, there are also Christmas candies, such as peppermint candy canes (elegant in all-white), ribbon candy, and a European favorite, marzipan. No wonder children have visions of sugarplums dancing in their heads!

The Thirteen Desserts of the Reveillon

I T IS THE CUSTOM in Provence, in the south of France, to have a feast on Christmas Eve—the *reveillon*—after midnight mass, which is capped by thirteen desserts, which represent Christ and the apostles. There are nuts and dried fruits—almonds, hazelnuts, raisins, and dried figs—that represent four orders of monks. There is sweet oil bread (*pompe à l'huile*), a latticed bread that must be broken by hand, not sliced with a knife, or it will bring bad luck. Other elements include prunes or dried peaches, dates, walnuts, mandarin oranges (or quince jelly), pears or oranges, black and white nougat, a winter melon, and black and white grapes. Often these are incorporated into tarts or cookies.

A CHRISTMAS TEA AND MORE

HE CONVIVIAL SPIRIT AT Christmas makes it a natural time for entertaining. It is a season for seeing old friends, reuniting with family, and broadening the circle to draw in new acquaintances. Planning a party, always a little daunting, somehow seems more appealing during the holidays, when the festive energy in the air infects us with an urge to draw up guest lists and devise menus. Entertaining need not be on a grand scale, however; the best parties are often smaller, informal affairs that let you and your guests relax and enjoy the company.

An ice skating party on a winter night, accompanied by a picnic hamper with a thermos of hot cocoa and cookies, is a wonderfully old-fashioned way to socialize. An evening of caroling encourages people to partake in another underappreciated activity: singing. Have everyone over afterward to warm up with hot spiced cider and old-time treats like popcorn balls and gingerbread men.

Children will delight in a Saturday afternoon cookie-making party. Make sugar or gingerbread cookie dough and provide cookie cutters, icing, sprinkles, jimmies, and candies. Poke a hole in the top of each cookie before baking to make them into ornaments to hang on the tree. Or create (or buy) a plain gingerbread house for the children to decorate with gumdrops, licorice sticks, and Necco wafers. For an adult version, host a cookie exchange, with each person bringing one kind of cookie and then interchanging with one another.

The quintessential Christmas gathering is a tree-trimming party, to which guests bring an ornament. Play carols old and new, and before you know it, guests will be singing along. These are the kinds of parties that are perfect for families to enjoy together.

For a more elegant party that is still easygoing, host an afternoon tea. This is the perfect excuse to get out your good china and silver, and put the emphasis on creating a beautiful table. A few desserts, such as a tangy lemon bundt cake, buttery shortbread or madeleines, individual tarts, and a sampling of Christmas cookies make a delectable spread, with tea and sherry as accompaniments. Sugar-dusted fruit and peaks of whipped cream lend an appropriately snowy flourish. The benefit of a buffet setting is that you can put out the food and then enjoy the party with everyone else. One exquisite special effect, such as the chandelier draped in Spanish moss (not diffi-

A chandelier draped in Spanish moss and glass icicles, RIGHT, *sets the stage for a magical tea party. Lemon bundt cake, sugared fruits, rock candy for sweetening the tea and a decanter of sherry are set on pedestals and trays to create a bountiful table. Tea makings,* ABOVE, *are set up on a dessert trolley.*

cult or expensive to achieve), will help the room—and the party—transcend the ordinary.

If you are not the plan-ahead type, keep a tray table or console set up with glasses and bar accoutrements and a few impromptu hors d'oeuvres (nuts, dried fruits, cheese, olives) on hand, and invite friends to drop by informally. Everything is at the ready when guests drop in, and it makes the house look particularly welcoming. Sherry and port can be put on display in shapely glass decanters, wreathed with rings of mistletoe, ivy, or boxwood for a sophisticated touch of holiday spirit.

Pure white candy canes, ABOVE, *without the familiar red stripes, have a surprising sophistication.* RIGHT: *Simple Shaker boxes and tins wait to be filled at a cookie-baking party in a country farmhouse.*

SETTING
THE TABLE

EFORE ANYONE has even taken a bite, the mood of a dinner or party has in large part been set—by the atmosphere, the mood, the intimacy of the setting. A beautifully set table is an invitation to join in the feast, to feel personally welcomed to a special occasion.

It starts with a place card—not a necessity, particularly at an informal dinner, but a thoughtful way to make each guest feel at home. Place cards can be purchased or easily made by hand: Cut out a seasonal shape from heavy paper or write guests' names in gold marker on a holly leaf; inscribe names in icing on Christmas cookies; use a rubber stamp or embosser to decorate plain card stock; or write names in beautiful script. Small table gifts are another gesture of welcome; they can be as simple as a tree ornament, a flower, or a tiny box of chocolates.

White is a stylish starting point for any table—it creates a clean backdrop to show off the food; it has an inherent elegance and classicism; it is pure and uncluttered. White works with a wide range of styles, not just starched linen and Victorian silver, but also the more modern look of a bare white table adorned with unassuming crates of paperwhites, clear glass plates, and simple goblets. White can also be romantic, with antique creamware in

A small calligraphy-emblazoned banner, ABOVE, *makes a charming place card accented with two bay leaves. The creamware and silver,* RIGHT, *are stacked on the table in preparation for a party.*

pierced and filigreed patterns, a profusion of roses in a silver tureen, and etched crystal stemware. White suits Christmas tables in particular because it never competes with the decorations; it offers a pocket of serenity. It is easy to work with because you can blend different place settings and service pieces, different styles and periods, even different shades—in fact, such variation adds interest, and the unified palette makes it all work together.

A table takes on character when it reflects your personal point of view. Take inspiration from what you already have—small silver picture frames for place cards, a collection of oil lanterns among greens to illuminate the table, vintage Christmas china mixed in with regular dinnerware, a damaged white quilt as a tablecloth. Flowers, fruits, and evergreens add life: A bare table could be blanketed with pine boughs or etched with bittersweet branches, with votive candles tucked in here and there. Sprigs of greenery can be tucked into napkins or used to wreathe plates. Instead of a large floral centerpiece, place a single bloom at each setting in a bud vase. Edible fruits such as pears and lady apples, apricots and champagne grapes could fill a compote or the tiers of an ironstone cake stand.

Table linens—crisp and elegant in white or ivory

—can range from a runner down the center of the table to a formal damask or embroidered tablecloth to large white napkins slipped through napkin rings and draped over the edge of the table. Hand embroidery and monograms, lace and cutwork, whether on your own linens or ones acquired at flea markets and estate sales, add the resonance of time and a touch

ears coated in sugar crystals, ABOVE, *apricots and pine needles festively fill glass pedestals.* RIGHT: *Collars of mistletoe, variegated ivy, and boxwood dress up decanters of brandy and sherry.*

of the personal to the setting. Lace tablecloths look especially beautiful atop a mahogany table; the dark wood highlights their airy designs. Making a special tablecloth for the holidays can create a one-of-a-kind setting, whether a white-on-white appliqué of holly leaves on a sheer cloth or an old linen cloth bordered in tiny pinecones that have been hot-glued onto the edge.

Resources

FOR A WHITE CHRISTMAS

Santa's Stocking Stuffers

Postcards and stamps

Champagne splits

Bath salts and sachets

Travel-size toiletries

Earrings or cuff links

Packets of tea and a strainer

Cookie cutters

Chocolates or jelly beans

Herbs

Small tools—a tape measure, dual-head screwdriver, mini-flashlight

A favorite recipe

Framed photographs

Book of crossword puzzles

Christmas ornaments

Little books

Fountain pen

Cassette tapes

Pocket calendar

Playing cards

Cocktail napkins

Film and developing mailers

Movie coupons

Seed packets and small flowerpots

Just for Children

Stickers

Watercolors

Rubber stamps and stamp pads

Jacks

Jump rope

Playing cards

Crayons and coloring books

Hand puppet

Slinky

Silly Putty

Wind-up toys

Mini Lego set

Doll furniture

Modeling clay

Paper dolls

Miniature cars and trucks

Superballs

Diary

Disposable camera

Masks

Stick-on stars

Santa Claus Around the World

O UR IMAGE of Santa Claus is derived largely from the imaginations of writer Clement C. Moore, who described this jolly old elf and his reindeer-drawn sleigh in his book-length poem "A Visit from St. Nicholas" in 1822, and the illustrator Thomas Nast, whose drawings of a rotund Santa with a flowing white beard for *Harper's Illustrated Weekly* firmly etched Santa Claus's personage in our mind. Before the nineteenth century, Dutch and German figures called "Belsnickel" and "Christkindel," who bear a strong resemblance to our Santa Claus, were said to travel along back roads delivering gifts, but also carrying a stick to discipline bad children. In America, these were merged into the figure of "Kriss Kringle" and eventually, Santa Claus.

In Italy, *La Befana,* an old woman who flies through the air on her broom, brings gifts to children on the eve of the Epiphany. A similar figure in Russia is called *Baboushka.*

In the Czech Republic, *Svaty Mikulas,* patron saint of children, is said to slide down from heaven on a golden cord. And in parts of France, *Tante Aria* rides through the countryside on a donkey bringing gifts, while the Dutch *Sinterklaas* arrives on a great white horse. Whatever his (or her) mode of transportation, children the world over are understandably captivated by the generosity of this mythical figure.

SNOW

Snowmen

Snowball fights

Snow forts

Snowflakes on tongues

Paper snowflakes

Snowflake stencils

Snow sprayed on windows

Icicles

Christmas Tales

No matter how many times we read them, whether aloud to children or on our own, these stories never tire, and still embody what we hold dear about Christmas:

A CHRISTMAS CAROL
by Charles Dickens

A VISIT FROM
ST. NICHOLAS
by Clement C. Moore

THE GIFT OF THE MAGI
by O. Henry

A CHILD'S CHRISTMAS
IN WALES
by Dylan Thomas

A CHRISTMAS MEMORY
by Truman Capote

THE SNOWMAN
by Raymond Briggs

THE LITTLE MATCH GIRL
by Hans Christian Andersen

LITTLE WOMEN
by Louisa May Alcott
(the first two chapters)

THE GOSPEL ACCORDING
TO ST. LUKE

Songs of Snow

To conjure up the feeling of snow, listen to one of these songs:

LET IT SNOW

I'M DREAMING OF
A WHITE CHRISTMAS

WINTER WONDERLAND

SILVER BELLS

THE CHRISTMAS SONG
*(Chestnuts Roasting
on an Open Fire)*

I'LL BE HOME FOR CHRISTMAS

JINGLE BELLS

IT'S BEGINNING TO LOOK
A LOT LIKE CHRISTMAS

Christmas Film Classics

When you're looking for a little Christmas spirit, rent one of these old holiday classics:

IT'S A WONDERFUL LIFE

MIRACLE ON 34TH STREET

A CHRISTMAS CAROL

THE BELLS OF ST. MARY'S

CHRISTMAS
IN CONNECTICUT

HOLIDAY AFFAIR

THE BISHOP'S WIFE

Bibliography

CHRISTMAS IN AMERICA: A HISTORY, *by* Penne L. Restad (Oxford University Press, 1995).

CLASSIC HOME DESSERTS, *by* Richard Sax (Chapters, 1994).

THE EVERYTHING CHRISTMAS BOOK (Bob Adams, 1994).

THE GREAT AMERICAN CHRISTMAS ALMANAC, *by* Irena Chalmers (Viking Studio Books, 1988).

MILLER'S TRADITIONAL ENGLISH CHRISTMAS, *by* Judith and Martin Miller (Mitchell Beazley, 1992).

Childhood Joys

Do you remember:

Opening up a little door each day on the Advent calendar

Playing a tinsel-winged angel in the Christmas pageant

Seeing the Nutcracker Suite ballet for the first time

Sneaking a candy cane from the Christmas tree

Writing and rewriting your list for Santa Claus

Getting to stay up late on Christmas Eve

Licking the beaters and eating the broken cookies

Driving through the neighborhood at night to see all the lights

Sitting on Santa's lap

Placing the animals around the crèche

Making construction paper chains for the tree

Watching *A Charlie Brown Christmas* on television

MY FAVORITE THINGS

The first snowfall

Frosty windows

Candlelight

Sugar-dusted shortbread

Vanilla tea

Pots of paperwhites

Winterberry wreaths

White flannel sheets

Mistletoe

Champagne

Silent snowflakes

Hanging your stocking on the mantel

Leaving milk and cookies for Santa

The thrill of coming down the stairs on Christmas morning

The pleasure of playing with new toys all afternoon long

Sugar Cookies

MAKES 3 DOZEN

8 TABLESPOONS (1 STICK)
   SALTED BUTTER, MELTED

1 CUP SUGAR

1 LARGE EGG

2 EGG YOLKS

1 TO 1½ CUPS ALL–PURPOSE
   FLOUR

½ TEASPOON BAKING SODA

PINCH OF SALT

ADDITIONAL SUGAR
   TO SPRINKLE ON COOKIES

Combine the butter and sugar and beat until creamy. Add the egg and egg yolks and beat well. In a separate bowl, mix together the flour, baking soda, and salt. Gradually add to the butter mixture, using only enough of the flour mixture to make a dough you can roll. Beat well until the mixture holds together. Form into two balls, wrap them in aluminum foil or waxed paper and refrigerate for several hours.

Preheat the oven to 400°F. Remove the dough from the refrigerator and roll out very thin on a floured board. Cut into shapes with cookie cutters, sprinkle with granulated sugar, and place on greased baking sheets.

Bake for 10 minutes, or until the cookies are just golden around the edges. Cool on wire rack or large plate.

*Collect cookie cutters in all shapes and sizes.
My favorites are Christmas trees,
stars, reindeer, hearts, teapots, candy canes.*

*Decorate with sprinkled natural brown sugar,
silver dots, or a sheer white sugar glaze.*

*With a store-bought tube of white icing
or your own recipe, make dots, stripes, plaids,
borders, or write names or greetings.*

Mrs. Foley's Shortbread

MAKES 2 DOZEN

1 CUP CONFECTIONERS' SUGAR

1 POUND (4 STICKS) SALTED
   BUTTER, SOFTENED

4½ CUPS ALL-PURPOSE FLOUR

Preheat the oven to 325°F. Blend the confectioners' sugar into the butter, and then gradually add the flour, 1 cup at a time. Dough will be very thick. Place dough on floured surface, pat down, and roll out ¼ to ½ inch thick. Cut into 2½-inch squares, and place on an ungreased baking sheet. Prick the top of each square with a fork. Bake at 325°F for 25 to 30 minutes; cookies should be pale on top, but golden brown on the bottom. Remove from oven and cool on wire racks. Store in an airtight container.

Shortbread can also be cut into special shapes for the holidays; stars, rounds, squares, hearts, bars.

Add chopped walnuts or hazelnuts, crystallized ginger or lemon rind for different flavors.

Use 2 rounds and sandwich with apricot jam and dust with confectioners' sugar.

Dust with confectioners' sugar over paper doilies to create lacy patterns or press a single almond into the center.

Package in silver tins or wooden Shaker boxes. Wrap in cellophane with raffia or ivory silk ribbons.

FROM HAVING TEA

Good Causes

Give a gift to these or a worthy charity in your area:

GOD'S LOVE WE DELIVER
212-865-4800

LITERACY VOLUNTEERS
OF AMERICA
315-445-8000

MEALS ON WHEELS
212-348-4344

NATIONAL TRUST FOR
HISTORIC PRESERVATION
202-588-6000

THE NATURE
CONSERVANCY
800-628-6860

NEW YORK
FOUNDLING HOSPITAL
212-633-9300

UNICEF
800-FOR-KIDS

CHILDREN'S
DEFENSE FUND
212-233-4000

AMERICAN
CANCER SOCIETY
800-227-2345

THE SNOW

The snow, in bitter cold
Fell all the night!
And we awoke to see
the garden white. . . .
F. Ann Elliott

Directory

Retail Stores

Aero
132 Spring Street
New York, NY 10012
212-966-1500
Modern and vintage glass, trays

Bell'occhio
8 Brady Street
San Francisco, CA 94103
415-864-4048
Unusual one-of-a-kind gifts,
pins, ribbons, potions

Black Hound
149 First Avenue
New York, NY 10003
212-979-9505
800-344-4417
Contemporary packaged cookies,
poached fruits, and food gifts

Calvin Klein Home
at Calvin Klein
654 Madison Avenue
New York, NY 10022
212-292-9000
Cashmere and wool throws,
glass hurricanes,
candles, home fragrance,
china, table linens

Christian Tortu
at Takashimaya
693 Fifth Avenue
New York, NY 10022
800-753-2038
Vases, flower bouquets,
mossy pots, and topiaries

Claudia Laub
7404 Beverly Boulevard
Los Angeles, CA 90036
213-931-1710
800-221-3728
Letterpress Christmas cards,
invitations, and notecards

Crate & Barrel
650 Madison Avenue
New York, NY 10022
212-308-0011
Well-designed tabletop
and home basics

Dulken & Derrick
12 West 21st Street
New York, NY 10010
212-929-3614
Silk and velvet flowers,
nosegays, bouquets

Hammond Candy Company
2550 West 29th Avenue
Denver, CO 80211
303-455-2320
Old-fashioned hard candies

The Homestead
223 East Main Street
Fredericksburg, TX 78624
810-997-5551
Vintage linens, china,
French and English accessories

Hyman Hendler
67 West 38th Street
New York, NY 10018
212-840-8393
Vintage and new ribbons—satin,
velvet, grosgrain, and wired

IKEA
For the store nearest you, call
800-434-4532.
Inexpensive Swedish tableware,
candles, and decorations

Manhattan Fruitier
105 East 29th Street
New York, NY 10016
212-686-0404
*Custom fruit baskets and
gourmet foods*

Ornamenta
235 Main Street
Northport, NY 11768
516-757-2949
Romantic accessories

Polo Country Store
31-33 Main Street
East Hampton, NY 11937
516-324-1222
Flannel sheets

Room Service
4354 Lovers Lane
Dallas, TX 75225
214-369-7666
*Fabrics, home furnishings, and
wonderful children's gifts*

Ruby Beets
Poxybogue Road & Route 27
Wainscott, NY 11932
516-537-2802
*Mercury glass, white ironstone,
painted vintage furniture, silver*

Tail of the Yak
2632 Ashby Avenue
Berkeley, CA 94705
510-841-9891
Unusual accessories, notebooks

Tender Buttons
143 East 62nd Street
New York, NY 10022
212-758-7004
Antique and vintage buttons

Terra Verde
120 Wooster Street
New York, NY 10012
212-925-4533
All-natural gifts

Treillage
420 East 75th Street
New York, NY 10021
212-535-2288
Garden pots, books, tools, furnishings

V.S.F. (Very Special Flowers)
204 West 10th Street
New York, NY 10011
212-206-7236
One-of-a-kind floral arrangements

COUNTRY SNOW SCENES

Church steeple in New England

Ice skating on frozen pond

Snowman with corncob pipe

CITY SNOW SCENES

Star at 57th Street & 5th Avenue

Central Park early morning

White lights down Park Avenue

Wolfman Gold & Good Co.
117 Mercer Street
New York, NY 10012
212-431-1888
All-white tablewares

Crate & Barrel
800-323-5461
*Candles and candleholders,
white tableware, and gifts*

Exposures
800-222-4947
Picture frames and scrapbooks

**Fredericksburg
Herb Farm**
800-259-4372
*Herb-scented candles, oils,
natural gifts*

Gardeners Eden
800-822-9600
Plants, pots, gifts for the gardener

Garnet Hill
800-622-6216
*Flannel sheets, duvets,
blankets, sleepwear*

Harry & David
800-547-3033
Fruit baskets and crates

The J. Peterman Company
1318 Russell Cave Road
Lexington, Kentucky 40505
800-231-7341 phone
800-346-3081 fax

L. L. Bean
800-341-4341
*Flannel sheets, wool blankets,
canvas log carriers*

Pottery Barn
800-922-9934
*Accessories for the home and
entertaining*

Smith & Hawken
800-776-3336
Wreaths, herb topiaries, accessories

Stamps by Mail
800-STAMPS-24
*Christmas stamps, bulk stamps,
and philatelic orders*

White Flower Farm
800-496-9600
*Paperwhite, amaryllis bulbs,
and other plants*

Williams-Sonoma
800-541-2233
Kitchen and gourmet gifts

THE WHITE CHRISTMAS SHOPPING LIST

Amaryllis bulbs
White Flower Farm
800-496-9600

Bags of paperwhite bulbs
White Flower Farm
800-496-9600

Bay leaf wreath
Smith & Hawken
800-776-3336

Big glass cylinders and candles
Calvin Klein Home
654 Madison Avenue
New York, NY 10022
212-292-9000

Boxes of white candles
IKEA
800-434-4532

Christmas cards, notes and invitations

Claudia Laub

7404 Beverly Boulevard

Los Angeles, CA 90036

213-931-1710, 800-221-3728

Classic creamware china

Bergdorf Goodman

754 Fifth Avenue

New York, NY 10022

212-753-7300

Cream flannel sheets

Garnet Hill, 800-622-6216

Fruit basket with flowers and biscotti

Manhattan Fruitier

105 East 29th Street

New York, NY 10016

212-686-0404

Ginger cookies

IKEA, 800-434-4532

Ivory cashmere throws

Calvin Klein Home

654 Madison Avenue

New York, NY 10022

212-292-9000

Ivory velvet roses

Dulken & Derrick

12 West 21st Street

New York, NY 10010

212-929-3614

Natural canvas log carrier and ice bags

L. L. Bean

800-922-9934

Off-white clay pots

G. Wolff Pottery

305 Litchfield Turnpike

New Preston, CT 06777

203-868-2858

Papers, ribbons, wraps

Kate's Paperie

561 Broadway

New York, NY 10012

212-941-9816

Pecan heart cookies in boxes

Black Hound

149 First Avenue

New York, NY 10003

212-979-9505

800-344-4417

Poached pears in glass jars

Black Hound

149 First Avenue

New York, NY 10003

212-979-9505

800-344-4417

Primitive ornaments

Nannyberry Antiques

32 MacArthur Avenue

Huntington, NY 11743

516-421-5491

Rosemary-scented candles

Fredericksburg Herb Farm

800-259-4372

Silk ribbons

Hyman Hendler

67 West 38th Street

New York, NY 10018

212-840-8393

Straw ornaments

IKEA, 800-434-4532

Vanilla tea

The Tea Box at Takashimaya

693 Fifth Avenue

New York, NY 10022

212-753-2038

White platters

Wolfman Gold & Good Co.

117 Mercer Street

New York, NY 10012

212-431-1888

Index